Trim The Fat
Weight Loss Simplified

Tiwayi Mushambi

Copyright © 2024 by Tiwayi Mushambi. All Right Reserved.

No part of this publication may be reproduced, distributed, or transmitted in any form or by any means, including photocopying, recording, or other electronic or mechanical methods, or by any information storage and retrieval system without the prior written permission of the publisher, except in the case of very brief quotations embodied in critical reviews and certain other noncommercial uses permitted by copyright law.

Why I Wrote This Book

ROI. APR. IPO. REIT. PIPE.

These are but a few of the acronyms and terms that are thrown around when it comes to investment banking. For a long time, they were intimidating and hard for the average person to grasp. The jargon and confusion served many investment bankers and money gurus well, because it helped them carve out a niche of dependent clients.

Now, there's an app for that. With the rise of Exchange Traded Funds(ETFs) and other democratized financial instruments, you don't even need to have intimate knowledge of individual stocks anymore. Just automate and wait. All of them work on the basic premise of buying low and selling high. However, the same cannot be said about the fitness industry.

If there is something that people desire more than wealth, it's health. There is not a single person on earth that would accept a billion dollars if it meant they wouldn't wake up the next day. This is what makes the fitness industry an infinite goldmine. There will always be people looking to get healthier.

The underlying factor that contributes to weight loss is the immutable first Law of Thermodynamics: Energy cannot be created or destroyed, but transformed. If you use more energy than you consume for long enough, your body will have no choice but to convert the energy stored in your body as fat. It's that simple.

But simplicity doesn't pay the bills. If we look at the economic impact of the fitness industry in the U.S., we find that it contributed more than 35 billion U.S. dollars to the U.S.

economy in 2021. That's a lot of dumbbells. Confusion is what keeps this machine alive, and every single sales person will swear that they found the best way to lose weight with minimal effort.

I never thought I'd ever see two health influencers argue over whether ice cream is healthier than fruits, but that's where it's gotten. Contradiction and controversial takes are the order of the day. The 'secret' to weight loss has always been known, but they need to obscure it in order to make their 'secret' more valuable.

Written with the average person in mind, this book cuts through the complex jungle of the fitness industry and provides clear and practical guidance. It covers essential topics such as calorie deficits, the role of steady state cardio, systematic fat loss strategies, and understanding energy balance.

Additionally, it delves into the benefits and considerations of intermittent fasting, the power of high fiber nutrition, and the importance of high protein nutrition. With a focus on creating a sustainable weight loss plan, overcoming common challenges, and maintaining long-term health, this book provides valuable insights and practical tips for achieving successful weight loss.

Even though we will go through various methods of fasting, eating and exercising, it is important to note that the only method that works is the one you execute consistently. The options presented are merely for you to select what you like and will perform continuously, even well after you achieve your goal weight.

So, let's cut through the B.S and trim the fat!

Enjoy your reading.

The Basics of Calorie Deficits

The best part about eating healthy is that you can fill your stomach without going over your calorie limit. For example, an entire watermelon has about 1300 calories, but you would be unable to take another bite for the rest of the day. 129 blueberries, 6 apricots and 100 blackberries (the fruit) are each just 100 calories!

When it comes to weight loss, one of the fundamental concepts to understand is the calorie deficit. A calorie deficit occurs when you consume fewer calories than your body needs to maintain its current weight, which averages to 2000 calories for women and 2500 calories for men. This creates an energy imbalance, forcing your body to tap into its stored fat reserves for fuel, ultimately leading to weight loss.

To grasp the concept of a calorie deficit, it's important to understand the role of calories in our bodies. Calories are units of energy that come from the food and beverages we consume. Our bodies require a certain amount of calories each day to perform basic functions such as breathing, digestion, and maintaining body temperature. This is known as our basal metabolic rate (BMR).

When we consume more calories than our body needs, the excess energy is stored as fat. On the other hand, when we consume fewer calories than our body needs, it starts using the stored fat as a source of energy, resulting in weight loss. This is the basic principle behind a calorie deficit.

Creating a calorie deficit can be achieved through a combination of diet and exercise. By reducing your calorie intake and increasing your physical activity, you can create an imbalance between the calories consumed and the calories burned.

To determine the appropriate calorie deficit for your weight loss goals, it's important to consider your current weight, activity level, and overall health. It's generally recommended to aim for a moderate calorie deficit of around 500 to 1000 calories per day. This gradual approach allows for sustainable weight loss without compromising your overall well-being.

It's important to note that extreme calorie deficits or crash diets are not recommended as they can lead to nutrient deficiencies, muscle loss, and a slower metabolism. The key is to find a balance that promotes steady and healthy weight loss.

To create a calorie deficit, you can start by tracking your daily calorie intake. This can be done by keeping a food diary or using a mobile app that allows you to log your meals and snacks. By becoming aware of your calorie consumption, you can identify areas where you may be overeating or making unhealthy food choices.

In addition to monitoring your calorie intake, incorporating regular physical activity into your routine is crucial for creating a calorie deficit. Exercise not only burns calories but also helps to increase your metabolism, build lean muscle mass, and improve overall fitness.

Steady state cardio, such as jogging, cycling, or swimming, is an effective way to burn calories and create a calorie deficit. This type of exercise involves maintaining a moderate intensity for an extended period of time, typically 30 minutes or more. It helps to elevate your heart rate and increase your calorie burn during and after the workout.

In combination with a calorie deficit, steady state cardio can contribute to significant weight loss over time. However, it's important to note that exercise alone is not enough to achieve sustainable weight loss. It should be complemented with a balanced and nutritious diet.

By understanding the basics of calorie deficits and incorporating them into your weight loss journey, you can take control of your health and achieve your desired goals. Remember, consistency and patience are key, as sustainable weight loss is a gradual process.

The Role of Steady State Cardio

The amount of calories you burn during a workout contribute approximately 20% of the total calories you burn during the day. Exercise is not your main contributor to the calorie deficit, so please do not injure yourself trying to burn 1000 calories in one thirty-minute sprint session. It is unsustainable.

Steady state cardio, also known as aerobic exercise, plays a crucial role in weight loss and overall fitness. It is a form of exercise that involves maintaining a steady and moderate intensity for an extended period of time. You know you are doing it right if you can still maintain a conversation while your heart is beating faster.

This type of cardio workout primarily targets the cardiovascular system, helping to improve heart health and increase endurance. In addition to its cardiovascular benefits, steady state cardio can also be an effective tool for burning calories and aiding in weight loss.

How Steady State Cardio Works

When engaging in steady state cardio, such as jogging, cycling, or swimming, your body relies on oxygen to produce energy. This energy is derived from the breakdown of carbohydrates and fats stored in your body. As you continue with the exercise, your heart rate increases, and your body starts to burn more calories to sustain the activity.

Steady state cardio is typically performed at a moderate intensity, where you can keep your pace without feeling overly breathless. This sustained effort allows your body to utilize oxygen efficiently and tap into its fat stores for energy. As a result, steady state cardio can contribute to fat loss and help you achieve a calorie deficit, which is essential for weight loss.

Benefits of Steady State Cardio

Calorie Burning: Steady state cardio is an effective way to burn calories during and after your workout. As you engage in aerobic exercise, your body continues to burn calories even after you've finished exercising.

This is known as the "afterburn effect" or excess post-exercise oxygen consumption (EPOC). By incorporating steady state cardio into your routine, you can increase your overall calorie expenditure and create a greater calorie deficit, leading to weight loss.

Improved Cardiovascular Health: Regular participation in steady state cardio can improve the health of your cardiovascular system. It strengthens your heart, increases lung capacity, and improves blood circulation. Over time, this can reduce the risk of heart disease, lower blood pressure, and improve overall cardiovascular fitness.

Increased Endurance: Steady state cardio helps to improve your endurance by training your body to sustain physical activity for longer periods. As you consistently engage in aerobic exercise, your body becomes more efficient at utilizing oxygen and delivering it to your muscles. This increased endurance can benefit various aspects of your life, from daily activities to sports performance.

Stress Reduction: Engaging in steady state cardio can have a positive impact on your mental well-being. It releases endorphins, which are known as "feel-good" hormones, and reduces stress hormones like cortisol. Regular exercise can help alleviate symptoms of anxiety and depression, improve mood, and enhance overall mental health.

Incorporating Steady State Cardio into Your Routine

To incorporate steady state cardio into your weight loss journey, consider the following tips:

Choose an Activity You Enjoy: Select an activity that you find enjoyable and can sustain for an extended period. This could be jogging, brisk walking, cycling, swimming, or using cardio machines like the elliptical or rowing machine. When you enjoy the activity, you are more likely to stick with it and make it a regular part of your routine.

Start Slow and Gradually Increase Intensity: If you're new to steady state cardio, start with shorter durations and lower intensities. Gradually increase the duration and intensity of your workouts as your fitness level improves. This approach will help prevent injuries and allow your body to adapt to the demands of aerobic exercise.

Include Variety: To prevent boredom and keep your workouts interesting, incorporate a variety of steady state cardio activities into your routine. This could include alternating between different forms of cardio or trying new activities altogether. Variety not only keeps you motivated but also challenges different muscle groups and prevents overuse injuries.

Combine with Strength Training: While steady state cardio is effective for burning calories and improving cardiovascular health, it is beneficial to combine it with strength training. Strength training helps build lean muscle mass, which can increase your metabolism and further contribute to weight loss. Aim for a well-rounded fitness routine that includes both cardio and strength training exercises.

Remember, consistency is key when it comes to steady state cardio. Aim for at least 150 minutes of moderate-intensity aerobic exercise per week, spread out over several days. Listen to your body, gradually increase the duration and intensity of your workouts, and enjoy the journey towards a healthier and fitter you.

In the next chapter, we will explore the concept of intermittent fasting and its potential impact on weight loss.

Systematic Fat Loss Strategies

Many people make the mistake of assuming that since you can build a specific muscle by concentrating on it, you can also lose fat in a specific area through targeted workouts. Let me be clear: spot reduction is a myth. It's like trying to drain one specific corner of a bathtub.

Drilling a hole in that area will drain the water, but the water will always be level, gradually decreasing until the bathtub is empty. That's how the body loses fat: systematically. Instead of spot training, focus on making your whole body move. You will burn more calories and grow stronger in the process.

When it comes to weight loss, having a systematic approach can make all the difference. By implementing effective fat loss strategies, you can optimize your efforts and achieve your goals more efficiently. In this section, we will explore some key strategies that can help you on your weight loss journey.

Set Realistic Goals

Before diving into any fat loss strategy, it's important to set realistic goals. Understanding what you want to achieve and having a clear vision of your desired outcome will provide you with the motivation and focus needed to stay on track. Setting realistic goals ensures that you don't set yourself up for disappointment or frustration.

When setting your goals, consider both short-term and long-term objectives. Short-term goals can help you stay motivated and provide a sense of accomplishment along the way. Long-term goals, on the other hand, give you a broader perspective and help you stay committed to your weight loss journey.

Create a Calorie Deficit

One of the fundamental principles of weight loss is creating a calorie deficit. This means consuming fewer calories than your body needs to maintain its current weight. By doing so, your body will tap into its fat stores to make up for the energy deficit, leading to weight loss.

To create a calorie deficit, you can either reduce your calorie intake through mindful eating or increase your calorie expenditure through physical activity. Ideally, a combination of both approaches is recommended for optimal results. Tracking your calorie intake and expenditure can be helpful in ensuring that you are consistently in a calorie deficit.

Incorporate Steady State Cardio

Incorporating steady state cardio into your fitness routine can help boost your metabolism, improve cardiovascular health, and enhance fat burning. Activities such as brisk walking, jogging, cycling, swimming, or using cardio machines at the gym are all great options for steady state cardio.

Implement Resistance Training

While steady state cardio is beneficial for weight loss, incorporating resistance training into your routine is equally important. Resistance training helps build lean muscle mass, which can increase your metabolism and improve your body composition.

When you engage in resistance training, your muscles undergo micro-tears, and during the recovery process, they become stronger and more toned. This increase in muscle mass leads to a higher resting metabolic rate, meaning you burn more calories even at rest.

Including exercises such as weightlifting, bodyweight exercises, or using resistance bands can help you build strength and promote fat loss. Aim to incorporate resistance training at least two to three times a week for optimal results.

Prioritize Sleep and Stress Management

Sleep and stress management play crucial roles in your weight loss journey. Lack of sleep and chronic stress can disrupt your hormone levels, increase cravings, and hinder your progress.

Aim to prioritize quality sleep by establishing a consistent sleep schedule and creating a relaxing bedtime routine. Getting adequate restorative sleep can help regulate your appetite hormones and support overall well-being.

Additionally, managing stress through techniques such as meditation, deep breathing exercises, or engaging in activities you enjoy can help reduce emotional eating and promote a healthier mindset.

Stay Consistent and Monitor Progress

Consistency is key when it comes to achieving sustainable weight loss. It's important to stay committed to your fat loss strategies and make them a part of your lifestyle. Remember that weight loss is a journey, and it takes time and effort to see significant results.

Monitoring your progress along the way can be motivating and help you make necessary adjustments to your strategies. Keep track of your weight, measurements, and how you feel both physically and mentally. Celebrate your achievements and use any setbacks as learning opportunities to refine your approach.

By implementing these systematic fat loss strategies, you can create a solid foundation for your weight loss journey. Remember to set realistic goals, create a calorie deficit, incorporate both steady state cardio and resistance training, prioritize sleep and stress management, and stay consistent. With dedication and perseverance, you can achieve your weight loss goals and improve your overall well-being.

Understanding Energy Balance

Energy balance refers to the relationship between the energy we consume through food and the energy we expend through physical activity and bodily functions. This balance ultimately determines whether we gain, maintain, or lose weight.

Energy Intake: Calories In

The first component of energy balance is energy intake, which refers to the calories we consume through our diet. Calories are a unit of measurement that quantifies the energy content of food and beverages. When we eat, our bodies break down the food and convert it into energy to fuel our daily activities.

Understanding the concept of calorie deficits, which was discussed in Chapter 1, is crucial in managing energy intake. A calorie deficit occurs when we consume fewer calories than our bodies need to maintain their current weight. This deficit forces our bodies to tap into stored fat for energy, leading to weight loss over time.

To create a calorie deficit, it is important to be mindful of the types and quantities of food we consume. Opting for nutrient-dense foods that are low in calories but high in essential nutrients can help us achieve a calorie deficit without compromising our overall health. Additionally, portion control and mindful eating practices can assist in managing energy intake effectively.

Energy Expenditure: Calories Out

The second component of energy balance is energy expenditure, which refers to the calories we burn through physical activity and bodily functions. Our bodies constantly require energy to perform essential functions such as breathing, circulating blood, and maintaining body temperature. This is known as our basal metabolic rate (BMR).

In addition to our BMR, physical activity and exercise contribute to our overall energy expenditure. Engaging in activities such as walking, running, strength training, and even household chores increases the number of calories we burn. The intensity and duration of these activities play a role in determining the total energy expenditure.

It is important to note that everyone's energy expenditure is unique and influenced by factors such as age, gender, body composition, and genetics. However, by incorporating regular physical activity into our daily routines, we can increase our energy expenditure and support weight loss efforts.

Achieving Energy Balance for Weight Loss

To achieve weight loss, it is necessary to create an energy imbalance by consuming fewer calories than we expend. This can be accomplished through a combination of managing energy intake and increasing energy expenditure.

By understanding the principles of calorie deficits and energy expenditure, we can make informed decisions about our diet and exercise routines. It is important to strike a balance between reducing calorie intake and increasing physical activity to ensure sustainable weight loss.

Tracking our calorie intake and expenditure can be a helpful tool in achieving energy balance. Various apps and online tools are available to assist in monitoring our food intake and physical activity levels. By keeping a record of our progress, we can identify patterns, make adjustments, and stay accountable to our weight loss goals.

The Role of Energy Balance in Weight Maintenance

Once we have achieved our desired weight loss, maintaining a healthy weight becomes the next challenge. Energy balance continues to play a crucial role in weight maintenance. It is important to find a balance between energy intake and expenditure that allows us to sustain our weight without regaining the lost pounds.

By understanding our individual energy needs and making mindful choices about our diet and physical activity, we can maintain a healthy weight in the long term. Regular monitoring and adjustments may be necessary to ensure that our energy balance remains in equilibrium.

In conclusion, understanding energy balance is essential for successful weight loss and weight maintenance. By creating a calorie deficit through managing energy intake and increasing energy expenditure, we can achieve our weight loss goals. Maintaining a balanced energy equation is key to sustaining a healthy weight and overall well-being.

Intermittent Fasting

Intermittent fasting has gained significant popularity in recent years as a weight loss strategy. It is not just a diet, but rather an eating pattern that involves alternating periods of fasting and eating. This approach to eating has been practiced for centuries and has shown promising results in terms of weight loss and overall health improvement.

Intermittent fasting works on the principle of restricting the time window in which you consume your meals. Instead of focusing on what you eat, it emphasizes when you eat. By incorporating periods of fasting into your daily routine, you can create a calorie deficit and promote fat burning.

How Intermittent Fasting Works

When you consume food, your body breaks it down into glucose, which is used as a primary source of energy. Any excess glucose that is not immediately needed is stored in the liver and muscles as glycogen. Once these glycogen stores are full, any additional glucose is converted into fat and stored in adipose tissue.

During periods of fasting, your body depletes its glycogen stores and starts relying on stored fat for energy. This metabolic shift promotes fat burning and can lead to weight loss. Additionally, intermittent fasting has been shown to have positive effects on insulin sensitivity, hormone regulation, and cellular repair processes.

Different Intermittent Fasting Methods

There are several different methods of intermittent fasting, each with its own unique approach to fasting and eating windows. Here are some of the most popular methods:

16/8 Method: This method involves fasting for 16 hours and restricting your eating window to 8 hours. For example, you might choose to eat between 12 pm and 8 pm, and then fast from 8 pm until 12 pm the next day.

5:2 Diet: With this method, you eat normally for five days of the week and restrict your calorie intake to 500-600 calories for the remaining two days. These fasting days should not be consecutive and can be spread throughout the week.

Alternate Day Fasting: As the name suggests, this method involves fasting every other day. On fasting days, you consume little to no calories, while on non-fasting days, you eat normally.

Eat-Stop-Eat: This method involves fasting for 24 hours once or twice a week. For example, you might choose to fast from dinner one day until dinner the next day.

Warrior Diet: This method involves fasting for 20 hours and eating one large meal within a 4-hour window. During the fasting period, small amounts of raw fruits and vegetables can be consumed.

Benefits and Considerations of Intermittent Fasting

Intermittent fasting offers several benefits beyond weight loss. Here are some of the key advantages:

Simplicity: Intermittent fasting is relatively easy to follow compared to other diets. It doesn't require counting calories or restricting specific food groups. Instead, it focuses on when you eat, making it a simple and flexible approach.

Weight Loss: By creating a calorie deficit, intermittent fasting can help you lose weight. It promotes fat burning and can lead to a reduction in overall body fat percentage.

Improved Insulin Sensitivity: Intermittent fasting has been shown to improve insulin sensitivity, which is crucial for maintaining stable blood sugar levels and preventing the development of type 2 diabetes.

Enhanced Autophagy: Autophagy is a cellular process that involves the removal of damaged cells and the recycling of cellular components. Intermittent fasting has been found to stimulate autophagy, which may have anti-aging and disease-preventing effects.

While intermittent fasting has many benefits, it may not be suitable for everyone. Consider the following factors before starting an intermittent fasting regimen:

Individual Differences: Each person's body and metabolism are unique. What works for one person may not work for another. It's important to listen to your body and adjust your fasting schedule accordingly.

Medical Conditions: If you have any underlying medical conditions or are taking medications, it's essential to consult with your healthcare provider before starting intermittent fasting. Certain conditions, such as diabetes or eating disorders, may require special considerations.

Nutritional Needs: It's crucial to ensure that you are meeting your nutritional needs during the eating window. Focus on consuming a balanced diet that includes a variety of nutrient-dense foods to support your overall health.

Implementing Intermittent Fasting in Your Routine

If you decide to try intermittent fasting, it's important to ease into it and find a method that suits your lifestyle. Here are some tips for implementing intermittent fasting in your routine:

Start Slowly: If you're new to fasting, begin with a shorter fasting window and gradually increase the duration as you become more comfortable. This will allow your body to adapt to the changes gradually.

Stay Hydrated: During fasting periods, it's important to stay hydrated. Drink plenty of water, herbal tea, or other non-caloric beverages to keep your body hydrated and help curb hunger.

Listen to Your Body: Pay attention to your hunger and fullness cues. If you feel excessively hungry or unwell during fasting periods, it may be a sign that the fasting window is too long for you. Adjust your fasting schedule accordingly.

Maintain a Balanced Diet: While intermittent fasting doesn't restrict specific foods, it's important to focus on consuming a balanced diet during your eating window. Include a variety of fruits, vegetables, whole grains, lean proteins, and healthy fats to meet your nutritional needs.

Remember, intermittent fasting is just one tool in your weight loss journey. It's important to combine it with other healthy lifestyle habits, such as regular exercise and mindful eating, to achieve sustainable and long-term weight loss success.

There are several different methods of intermittent fasting, each with its own unique approach and benefits. In this section, we will explore some of the most common intermittent fasting methods and how they can be implemented into your weight loss journey.

The 16/8 Method

The 16/8 method is one of the most popular and simplest forms of intermittent fasting. It involves fasting for 16 hours and restricting your eating window to 8 hours each day. This method can be easily incorporated into your daily routine by skipping breakfast and having your first meal around noon, then eating your last meal of the day by 8 pm. During the fasting period, you can consume calorie-free beverages such as water, black coffee, or herbal tea to help curb hunger.

The 16/8 method is flexible and can be adjusted to suit your lifestyle. For example, you can choose to fast from 8 pm to 12 pm the next day or from 9 pm to 1 pm. It is important to listen to your body and find a fasting window that works best for you. During the eating window, it is crucial to focus on consuming nutrient-dense foods that support your weight loss goals.

The 5:2 Method

The 5:2 method involves eating normally for five days of the week and restricting calorie intake to 500-600 calories for the remaining two days. On the fasting days, it is recommended to spread the calorie intake throughout the day by having small meals or snacks. For example, you can have a light breakfast, a small lunch, and a light dinner to meet the calorie restriction.

The 5:2 method allows for more flexibility in terms of when the fasting days are scheduled. Some people prefer to have their fasting days consecutively, such as on Mondays and Thursdays, while others prefer to space them out throughout the week. It is important to note that on non-fasting days, it is essential to maintain a balanced and healthy diet to support overall well-being.

Alternate Day Fasting

Alternate day fasting involves alternating between fasting days and regular eating days. On fasting days, calorie intake is significantly reduced or eliminated altogether, while on regular eating days, you can consume your usual amount of calories. This method can be more challenging for some individuals, as it requires a higher level of discipline and self-control.

There are different variations of alternate day fasting, such as the modified version, where you consume a limited number of calories (around 500-600) on fasting days instead of completely fasting. This can make the fasting days more manageable and sustainable for some individuals.

Eat-Stop-Eat

The Eat-Stop-Eat method involves fasting for 24 hours once or twice a week. This means that you would have dinner one day and then fast until dinner the next day. During the fasting period, it is important to stay hydrated and consume calorie-free beverages to help manage hunger.

This method can be challenging for beginners, as it involves a longer fasting period. It is recommended to start with shorter fasting periods and gradually increase the duration as your body adapts. It is also important to listen to your body and ensure that you are getting adequate nutrition on non-fasting days.

The Warrior Diet

The Warrior Diet is based on the concept of eating one large meal at night, following a period of fasting throughout the day. During the fasting period, small amounts of raw fruits and vegetables, as well as protein-rich snacks, can be consumed. The main meal is typically consumed within a 4-hour window in the evening.

This method is inspired by the eating patterns of ancient warriors and is designed to align with the body's natural circadian rhythm. Advocates of the Warrior Diet claim that it can improve energy levels, mental clarity, and overall well-being. However, it is important to ensure that the main meal is balanced and provides all the necessary nutrients.

The OMAD (One Meal a Day) Diet

The OMAD diet involves fasting for 23 hours and consuming all your daily calories within a 1-hour eating window. This method is highly restrictive and requires careful planning to ensure that you are meeting your nutritional needs within a single meal. It is crucial to focus on consuming a well-balanced meal that includes protein, healthy fats, complex carbohydrates, and a variety of fruits and vegetables.

The OMAD diet may not be suitable for everyone, especially those with specific dietary requirements or medical conditions. It is important to consult with a healthcare professional or registered dietitian before embarking on this type of fasting method.

Choosing the Right Method for You

When considering intermittent fasting, it is important to choose a method that aligns with your lifestyle, preferences, and overall health. It is also crucial to listen to your body and make adjustments as needed. Some individuals may find certain methods more sustainable and effective than others.

Experimenting with different intermittent fasting methods can help you find the approach that works best for you. It is important to remember that intermittent fasting is not a one-size-fits-all solution, and what works for one person may not work for another. It is always recommended to consult with a healthcare professional or registered dietitian before making any significant changes to your eating patterns or embarking on a new weight loss strategy.

In the next section, we will explore the benefits and considerations of intermittent fasting, helping you make an informed decision about incorporating it into your weight loss journey.

Benefits and Considerations of

Intermittent Fasting

Intermittent fasting has gained significant popularity in recent years as a weight loss strategy. It involves alternating periods of fasting and eating within a specific time window. While it may seem counterintuitive to skip meals in order to lose weight, intermittent fasting offers several benefits and considerations that make it an effective approach for many individuals.

Improved Insulin Sensitivity

One of the key benefits of intermittent fasting is its positive impact on insulin sensitivity. Insulin is a hormone that regulates blood sugar levels and plays a crucial role in fat storage. When we consume food, especially carbohydrates, our body releases insulin to help transport glucose into cells for energy. However, in a state of constant eating, our body becomes less sensitive to insulin, leading to higher insulin levels and increased fat storage.

Intermittent fasting helps improve insulin sensitivity by allowing our body to have longer periods without food. During the fasting period, our insulin levels decrease, and our body becomes more efficient at utilizing stored fat for energy. This can lead to a reduction in overall body fat and improved metabolic health.

Enhanced Fat Burning

Another significant benefit of intermittent fasting is its ability to enhance fat burning. When we fast, our body depletes its glycogen stores, which are the stored form of glucose. Once these stores are depleted, our body switches to burning fat for energy. This process, known as ketosis, can lead to increased fat oxidation and ultimately contribute to weight loss.

Intermittent fasting also increases the production of growth hormone, which plays a role in fat metabolism. Higher levels of growth hormone can help preserve lean muscle mass while promoting the breakdown of stored fat. This can result in a more favorable body composition and a higher metabolic rate.

Simplified Eating Patterns

One of the reasons why intermittent fasting has become so popular is its simplicity. Unlike other dieting approaches that require strict calorie counting or complicated meal plans, intermittent fasting simplifies eating patterns. By restricting the eating window, individuals can focus on consuming nutritious meals during a specific time frame, rather than constantly worrying about what and when to eat.

This simplicity can make intermittent fasting more sustainable in the long term. It eliminates the need for constant meal preparation and allows for more flexibility in daily routines. Many people find it easier to adhere to a specific eating window rather than constantly monitoring their food intake throughout the day.

Potential Health Benefits

In addition to weight loss, intermittent fasting has been associated with several potential health benefits. Research suggests that intermittent fasting may improve cardiovascular health by reducing blood pressure, cholesterol levels, and markers of inflammation. It may also enhance brain health and improve cognitive function.

Intermittent fasting has also shown promise in reducing the risk of chronic diseases such as type 2 diabetes and certain types of cancer. While more research is needed to fully understand the long-term effects, the initial findings are promising and suggest that intermittent fasting may have broader health benefits beyond weight loss.

Considerations and Precautions

While intermittent fasting can be an effective weight loss strategy, it may not be suitable for everyone. It is important to consider individual circumstances and consult with a healthcare professional before starting any fasting regimen. Some considerations and precautions include:

Nutrient Adequacy

During the eating window, it is crucial to ensure that the body receives adequate nutrients. Since the eating window is often shorter, it is important to focus on consuming nutrient-dense foods that provide essential vitamins, minerals, and macronutrients. A well-balanced diet that includes a variety of fruits, vegetables, whole grains, lean proteins, and healthy fats is essential to meet nutritional needs.

Potential Disruption of Eating Patterns

Intermittent fasting may disrupt social eating patterns, especially during the fasting period. It is important to consider how fasting may impact social interactions and plan accordingly. Communicating with friends and family about your fasting schedule can help manage expectations and ensure a supportive environment.

Individual Variations and Adaptation

Every individual is unique, and what works for one person may not work for another. It is important to listen to your body and make adjustments as needed. Some individuals may find it challenging to adapt to intermittent fasting initially, while others may experience positive effects right away. Experimenting with different fasting protocols and finding what works best for you is key to long-term success.

Potential Discomfort and Hunger

During the fasting period, it is common to experience hunger and discomfort, especially in the beginning. However, these sensations often subside as the body adapts to the fasting routine. Staying well-hydrated, consuming calorie-free beverages, and keeping busy can help manage hunger pangs and discomfort during fasting periods.

In conclusion, intermittent fasting offers several benefits for weight loss and overall health. It can improve insulin sensitivity, enhance fat burning, simplify eating patterns, and potentially provide additional health benefits.

However, it is important to consider individual circumstances, ensure nutrient adequacy, and listen to your body when implementing intermittent fasting as a weight loss strategy. With proper planning and guidance, intermittent fasting can be a powerful tool in achieving sustainable weight loss and improving overall well-being.

Getting Started with Intermittent Fasting

Now that you have a better understanding of the different intermittent fasting methods, it's time to implement it into your routine. Here are some steps to help you get started:

Choose the Right Method: Consider your lifestyle, work schedule, and personal preferences when selecting an intermittent fasting method. Pick one that aligns with your daily routine and is sustainable in the long run.

Start Slowly: If you're new to intermittent fasting, it's best to ease into it gradually. Begin by extending your overnight fast by skipping breakfast or delaying your first meal. As your body adapts, you can gradually increase the fasting window.

Stay Hydrated: During fasting periods, it's important to stay hydrated. Drink plenty of water, herbal tea, or other non-caloric beverages to keep your body hydrated and help curb hunger.

Listen to Your Body: Pay attention to your body's hunger and fullness cues. Intermittent fasting should not be a punishment, but rather a way to develop a healthier relationship with food. If you feel excessively hungry or unwell, adjust your fasting window or seek guidance from a healthcare professional.

Plan Your Meals: When it's time to break your fast, focus on consuming nutrient-dense foods that provide essential vitamins, minerals, and macronutrients. Include a balance of lean proteins, whole grains, fruits, vegetables, and healthy fats in your meals to support your overall health and weight loss goals.

Be Consistent: Consistency is key when it comes to intermittent fasting. Stick to your chosen fasting and eating windows as much as possible to allow your body to adapt and experience the full benefits of this eating pattern.

Combining Intermittent Fasting with Other Strategies

Intermittent fasting can be a powerful tool on its own, but it can also be combined with other weight loss strategies to enhance results. Here are a few strategies you can consider:

Calorie Deficit: Intermittent fasting can help create a calorie deficit by reducing the number of meals and snacks consumed throughout the day. However, it's still important to ensure that you're consuming an appropriate number of calories to support your weight loss goals. Calculate your daily calorie needs and adjust your meal sizes accordingly.

Steady State Cardio: Incorporating steady state cardio exercises, such as brisk walking, jogging, or cycling, into your routine can further enhance the effects of intermittent fasting. Engaging in cardio exercises during your fasting period can help burn stored fat for energy and accelerate weight loss.

High Fiber, High Protein Nutrition: Pairing intermittent fasting with a diet rich in fiber and protein can help you feel fuller for longer and support your weight loss efforts. Include plenty of fruits, vegetables, whole grains, lean meats, legumes, and nuts in your meals to ensure you're getting an adequate intake of these essential nutrients.

Remember, it's important to consult with a healthcare professional or registered dietitian before starting any new diet or fasting regimen, especially if you have any underlying health conditions or concerns.

Implementing intermittent fasting into your routine can be a game-changer in your weight loss journey. By choosing the right method, starting slowly, and combining it with other effective strategies, you can achieve sustainable weight loss and improve your overall health and well-being. Stay committed, be patient, and enjoy the benefits that intermittent fasting can bring to your life.

The Role of Fiber in Weight Loss

Fiber is an essential component of a healthy diet that plays a crucial role in weight loss. While it may not be as glamorous as other weight loss strategies, such as calorie deficits or intermittent fasting, the inclusion of fiber in your diet can have a significant impact on your weight loss journey. In this section, we will explore the various ways in which fiber aids in weight loss and how you can incorporate fiber-rich foods into your diet.

Understanding the Benefits of Fiber

Fiber is a type of carbohydrate that cannot be digested by the body. It passes through the digestive system relatively intact, adding bulk to the stool and aiding in regular bowel movements. However, its benefits extend far beyond promoting healthy digestion.

One of the primary benefits of fiber is its ability to create a feeling of fullness or satiety. When you consume foods high in fiber, they take longer to chew and digest, which can help you feel satisfied for longer periods. This can be particularly beneficial for individuals who struggle with overeating or snacking between meals. By including fiber-rich foods in your diet, you can reduce the overall calorie intake without feeling deprived.

Another advantage of fiber is its impact on blood sugar levels. Foods high in fiber, such as whole grains, legumes, and vegetables, have a lower glycemic index, meaning they cause a slower and more gradual rise in blood sugar levels. This can help stabilize blood sugar levels and prevent spikes and crashes, which can lead to cravings and overeating.

Furthermore, fiber-rich foods are generally lower in calorie density. This means that they contain fewer calories per gram compared to foods that are low in Fiber. By incorporating more fiber into your meals, you can increase the volume of food you consume without significantly increasing the calorie content. This can help you feel satisfied while still maintaining a calorie deficit, which is essential for weight loss.

Types of Fiber and Their Effects

There are two main types of dietary fiber: soluble fiber and insoluble fiber. Both types are beneficial for weight loss, but they have slightly different effects on the body.

Soluble fiber dissolves in water and forms a gel-like substance in the digestive tract. This type of fiber can help lower cholesterol levels and regulate blood sugar levels. Good sources of soluble fiber include oats, barley, legumes, fruits, and vegetables.

Insoluble fiber, on the other hand, does not dissolve in water and adds bulk to the stool. It helps promote regular bowel movements and prevents constipation. Foods rich in insoluble fiber include whole grains, nuts, seeds, and the skin of fruits and vegetables.

To maximize the benefits of fiber for weight loss, it is important to consume a variety of both soluble and insoluble Fiber. This can be achieved by incorporating a wide range of Fiber-rich foods into your diet.

How Fiber Supports Weight Loss

The inclusion of fiber in your weight loss plan can have several positive effects on your overall progress. Here are some ways in which fiber supports weight loss:

1. Increased Satiety

As mentioned earlier, fiber-rich foods take longer to chew and digest, which can help you feel fuller for longer periods. By increasing the volume of food without significantly increasing the calorie content, fiber can help reduce overall calorie intake and prevent overeating.

2. Reduced Calorie Absorption

Fiber can bind to some of the calories in the foods you consume, preventing their complete absorption by the body. This means that you may absorb fewer calories from a meal that contains a significant amount of fiber compared to a meal without Fiber.

3. Slower Digestion and Stabilized Blood Sugar Levels

Fiber slows down the digestion process, which can help regulate blood sugar levels and prevent spikes and crashes. By stabilizing blood sugar levels, fiber can reduce cravings and the likelihood of consuming high-calorie, sugary foods.

4. Improved Gut Health

Fiber acts as a prebiotic, providing nourishment for the beneficial bacteria in your gut. A healthy gut microbiome is essential for overall health and can contribute to weight loss. By promoting a healthy balance of gut bacteria, fiber can support digestion and nutrient absorption.

Incorporating Fiber-Rich Foods into Your Diet

Now that you understand the importance of fiber in weight loss, it's time to incorporate fiber-rich foods into your diet. Here are some tips to help you increase your fiber intake:

Choose whole grains: Opt for whole grain bread, pasta, and rice instead of their refined counterparts. These whole grains are higher in fiber and provide more nutrients.

Eat plenty of fruits and vegetables: Include a variety of fruits and vegetables in your meals and snacks. These are excellent sources of both soluble and insoluble Fiber.

Include legumes in your diet: Legumes, such as beans, lentils, and chickpeas, are rich in fiber and protein. They can be added to soups, salads, or used as a meat substitute in various dishes.

Snack on nuts and seeds: Nuts and seeds, such as almonds, chia seeds, and flaxseeds, are not only high in fiber but also provide healthy fats and protein. They make for a satisfying and nutritious snack.

Be mindful of portion sizes: While fiber is beneficial for weight loss, it's important to be mindful of portion sizes. Gradually increase your fiber intake to allow your body to adjust and prevent any digestive discomfort.

By incorporating these Fiber-rich foods into your diet, you can enhance your weight loss efforts and improve your overall health.

Remember, it's always important to stay hydrated when increasing your fiber intake. Drink plenty of water throughout the day to help the fiber move through your digestive system smoothly.

In the next section, we will explore some delicious Fiber-rich recipes that you can incorporate into your weight loss meal plan.

Fiber-Rich Foods and Recipes

Incorporating Fiber-rich foods into your diet is an essential component of a successful weight loss journey. Not only does fiber provide numerous health benefits, but it also plays a crucial role in promoting satiety, regulating blood sugar levels, and improving digestive health. In this section, we will explore the importance of fiber in weight loss and provide you with a variety of delicious Fiber-rich foods and recipes to help you achieve your goals.

Fiber-Rich Foods

Incorporating Fiber-rich foods into your diet is easier than you might think. Here are some excellent sources of dietary fiber that you can include in your meals:

1. Fruits and Vegetables

Fruits and vegetables are not only rich in vitamins and minerals but also high in Fiber. Some Fiber-rich options include apples, pears, berries, broccoli, Brussels sprouts, carrots, and leafy greens. Aim to include a variety of colorful fruits and vegetables in your diet to maximize your fiber intake.

2. Whole Grains

Swap refined grains for whole grains to increase your fiber intake. Whole grain options such as oats, quinoa, brown rice, whole wheat bread, and whole wheat pasta are excellent choices. These foods provide more fiber and nutrients compared to their refined counterparts.

3. Legumes

Legumes, including beans, lentils, chickpeas, and split peas, are not only a great source of plant-based protein but also packed with Fiber. Incorporate legumes into your meals by adding them to soups, salads, or making delicious bean-based dishes.

4. Nuts and Seeds

Nuts and seeds are not only a good source of healthy fats but also provide a decent amount of Fiber. Almonds, chia seeds, flaxseeds, and sunflower seeds are excellent options to include in your diet. Sprinkle them on top of salads, yogurt, or enjoy them as a snack.

Fiber-Rich Recipes

Here are a few Fiber-rich recipes to inspire you on your weight loss journey:

1. Quinoa and Vegetable Stir-Fry

Ingredients:

1 cup cooked quinoa

Assorted vegetables (broccoli, bell peppers, carrots, snap peas)

1 tablespoon olive oil

2 cloves garlic, minced

2 tablespoons low-sodium soy sauce

Instructions:

Heat olive oil in a pan over medium heat. Add minced garlic and sauté for a minute.

Add the vegetables and stir-fry until they are tender-crisp.

Add the cooked quinoa and soy sauce to the pan. Stir well to combine and heat through.

Serve hot and enjoy a delicious and Fiber-rich meal.

2. Chickpea Salad

Ingredients:

1 can chickpeas, drained and rinsed

1 cucumber, diced

1 tomato, diced

1/4 red onion, thinly sliced

1/4 cup chopped fresh parsley

Juice of 1 lemon

2 tablespoons olive oil

Salt and pepper to taste

Instructions:

In a large bowl, combine the chickpeas, cucumber, tomato, red onion, and parsley.

In a separate small bowl, whisk together the lemon juice, olive oil, salt, and pepper.

Pour the dressing over the chickpea mixture and toss to combine.

Refrigerate for at least 30 minutes to allow the flavors to meld together.

Serve chilled and enjoy a refreshing and Fiber-packed salad.

Incorporating High fiber Nutrition into Your Diet

To incorporate high fiber nutrition into your diet, consider the following tips:

Gradually increase your fiber intake: Start by adding small amounts of Fiber-rich foods to your meals and gradually increase the portion sizes. This will allow your body to adjust to the increased fiber intake without causing digestive discomfort.

Stay hydrated: fiber absorbs water, so it's important to drink an adequate amount of water throughout the day. Aim for at least 8 cups of water daily to support healthy digestion and prevent constipation.

Read food labels: When grocery shopping, read the nutrition labels to identify foods that are high in Fiber. Look for products that contain whole grains, fruits, vegetables, and legumes.

Plan your meals: Incorporate Fiber-rich foods into your meal planning. Include a variety of fruits, vegetables, whole grains, and legumes in your recipes to ensure a well-rounded and Fiber-packed diet.

Remember, it's important to consult with a healthcare professional or registered dietitian before making any significant changes to your diet, especially if you have any underlying health conditions or dietary restrictions.

Incorporating Fiber-rich foods into your diet is a simple and effective way to support your weight loss goals. By including a variety of fruits, vegetables, whole grains, and legumes, you can enjoy delicious meals while reaping the numerous health benefits of Fiber. So, start incorporating these Fiber-rich foods and recipes into your diet today and take a step closer to achieving your weight loss goals.

Understanding Protein and its Benefits

Who, what, when, where and Whey? Protein is an essential macronutrient that plays a crucial role in our overall health and well-being. When it comes to weight loss, protein is often hailed as the king of nutrients. It is not only important for building and repairing tissues but also for supporting various functions in the body.

In this section, we will delve deeper into the understanding of protein and its benefits in the context of weight loss.

What is Protein?

Protein is made up of amino acids, which are the building blocks of our body. These amino acids are responsible for the growth, repair, and maintenance of our muscles, organs, and other tissues. Unlike carbohydrates and fats, our body does not store protein, so it is important to consume it regularly to meet our daily needs.

The Role of Protein in Weight Loss

Protein plays a crucial role in weight loss for several reasons. Firstly, it has a high thermic effect, which means that our body burns more calories to digest and process protein compared to carbohydrates and fats. This increased calorie burn can contribute to a higher metabolic rate, making it easier to create a calorie deficit.

Secondly, protein is highly satiating, meaning it helps to keep us feeling full and satisfied for longer periods. This can be particularly beneficial when trying to reduce calorie intake and control hunger cravings. By including protein-rich foods in our meals and snacks, we can curb our appetite and prevent overeating.

Furthermore, protein is essential for preserving lean muscle mass during weight loss. When we restrict calories, our body may break down muscle tissue for energy. However, consuming an adequate amount of protein can help to minimize muscle loss and promote fat loss instead. This is important because maintaining muscle mass can help to keep our metabolism elevated and improve body composition.

Protein-Rich Foods and Recipes

Including protein-rich foods in our diet is essential for meeting our daily protein needs. Some excellent sources of protein include lean meats, poultry, fish, eggs, dairy products, legumes, nuts, and seeds. These foods not only provide us with high-quality protein but also offer other important nutrients such as vitamins, minerals, and healthy fats.

Here are a few examples of protein-rich recipes that you can incorporate into your weight loss journey:

- Grilled chicken breast with roasted vegetables
- Greek yogurt with berries and a sprinkle of nuts
- Lentil and vegetable stir-fry
- Baked salmon with quinoa and steamed greens
- Egg white omelet with spinach and feta cheese

These recipes are not only delicious but also provide a good balance of protein, carbohydrates, and healthy fats to support your weight loss goals.

Calculating Protein Needs for Weight Loss

Determining your protein needs for weight loss depends on various factors such as your age, gender, activity level, and overall health. As a general guideline, it is recommended to consume around 0.8 to 1 gram of protein per kilogram of body weight. However, if you are physically active or have specific dietary requirements, you may need to adjust your protein intake accordingly.

To calculate your protein needs, multiply your weight in kilograms by the recommended protein intake range. For example, if you weigh 70 kilograms, you would aim to consume between 56 to 70 grams of protein per day. It is important to spread your protein intake evenly throughout the day to optimize muscle protein synthesis.

Incorporating High Protein Nutrition into Your Diet

Incorporating high protein nutrition into your diet can be done in several ways. Here are some practical tips to help you increase your protein intake:

Start your day with a protein-rich breakfast such as eggs, Greek yogurt, or a protein smoothie.

Include a source of protein in each meal and snack. This can be lean meats, fish, poultry, tofu, legumes, or dairy products.

Opt for protein-rich snacks such as nuts, seeds, protein bars, or cottage cheese.

Experiment with plant-based protein sources like quinoa, lentils, chickpeas, and edamame.

Consider using protein supplements such as whey protein powder or plant-based protein powders if needed.

Remember, while protein is important for weight loss, it is still essential to maintain a balanced diet that includes a variety of nutrient-dense foods. Aim to combine protein with complex carbohydrates, healthy fats, and plenty of fruits and vegetables to ensure you are getting all the necessary nutrients for optimal health.

In conclusion, understanding the role of protein and its benefits in weight loss is crucial for achieving your goals. By including protein-rich foods in your diet, you can support muscle growth, increase satiety, and boost your metabolism. So, make sure to prioritize protein as a key component of your weight loss journey.

Setting Realistic Goals

Setting realistic goals is an essential step in creating a sustainable weight loss plan. Without clear and achievable goals, it can be challenging to stay motivated and track your progress effectively. In this section, we will discuss the importance of setting realistic goals and provide you with practical tips to help you set and achieve them.

Why Setting Realistic Goals Matters

When it comes to weight loss, setting realistic goals is crucial for several reasons. Firstly, unrealistic goals can lead to frustration and disappointment if they are not achieved within a specific timeframe. This can demotivate you and make it harder to stick to your weight loss plan in the long run.

Secondly, setting unrealistic goals may push you to adopt extreme measures or crash diets that are not sustainable or healthy. Rapid weight loss can have negative effects on your overall well-being and may result in muscle loss, nutrient deficiencies, and a slowed metabolism.

Lastly, setting realistic goals allows you to celebrate small victories along the way. By breaking down your weight loss journey into achievable milestones, you can stay motivated and maintain a positive mindset throughout the process.

Tips for Setting Realistic Goals

Be specific: Instead of setting a vague goal like "I want to lose weight," be specific about how much weight you want to lose and by when. For example, "I want to lose 10 pounds in the next three months."

Consider your lifestyle: Take into account your daily routine, work commitments, and personal responsibilities when setting your goals. Ensure that your weight loss plan is realistic and fits seamlessly into your lifestyle.

Set both short-term and long-term goals: Break down your weight loss journey into smaller, achievable goals. This will help you stay motivated and give you a sense of accomplishment along the way. For example, set a short-term goal of losing 2 pounds per week and a long-term goal of reaching your target weight within six months.

Focus on non-scale victories: While weight loss is often measured by the number on the scale, it's essential to recognize other indicators of progress. Celebrate non-scale victories such as increased energy levels, improved sleep, and fitting into smaller clothing sizes.

Make your goals measurable: Set goals that can be measured and tracked. For example, instead of saying "I want to exercise more," set a goal of exercising for 30 minutes, five days a week.

Be realistic about the timeline: Understand that weight loss is a gradual process and that sustainable results take time. Avoid setting unrealistic deadlines that may lead to disappointment or unhealthy behaviors.

Consult a healthcare professional: If you have significant weight loss goals or underlying health conditions, it's advisable to consult a healthcare professional or a registered dietitian. They can provide personalized guidance and help you set realistic goals based on your individual needs.

Stay flexible: Be open to adjusting your goals as you progress. Your body may respond differently than expected, and it's important to adapt your plan accordingly. Embrace the journey and be willing to make changes along the way.

Visualizing Your Goals

In addition to setting realistic goals, visualizing your goals can be a powerful tool in achieving success. Visualization involves creating a mental image of yourself at your desired weight and imagining how you will feel and look once you reach your goal.

To visualize your goals effectively, follow these steps:

Create a vision board: Gather images, quotes, and words that represent your weight loss goals and create a vision board. Place it somewhere visible, such as your bedroom or office, to remind yourself of your aspirations daily.

Practice guided imagery: Find a quiet and comfortable space, close your eyes, and imagine yourself at your ideal weight. Visualize the activities you will engage in, the clothes you will wear, and the confidence you will exude. Engage all your senses to make the visualization experience more vivid.

Use affirmations: Repeat positive affirmations related to your weight loss goals daily. For example, say statements like "I am capable of reaching my ideal weight" or "I am committed to making healthy choices." Affirmations can help reprogram your subconscious mind and reinforce your belief in your ability to achieve your goals.

Remember, visualization is a powerful tool, but it should be complemented by consistent action and a well-designed weight loss plan. Use visualization as a motivational tool to keep you focused and determined on your journey.

Setting realistic goals is the foundation of a successful weight loss plan. By being specific, considering your lifestyle, and staying flexible, you can set achievable goals that will keep you motivated and on track. Combine goal setting with visualization techniques to enhance your motivation and increase your chances of long-term success.

Staying Motivated and Overcoming Plateaus

When embarking on a weight loss journey, it is common to experience periods of plateau or a lack of progress. These plateaus can be frustrating and demotivating, but it is important to remember that they are a normal part of the process.

In this section, we will discuss strategies to stay motivated and overcome plateaus, ensuring that you continue to make progress towards your weight loss goals.

Set Realistic Expectations

One of the key factors in staying motivated is setting realistic expectations for your weight loss journey. It is important to understand that weight loss is not a linear process and that progress may vary from week to week.

Instead of focusing solely on the number on the scale, consider other indicators of progress such as how your clothes fit, improvements in energy levels, or changes in body composition.

By setting realistic expectations and acknowledging that progress may not always be immediate, you can maintain a positive mindset and stay motivated throughout your journey.

Celebrate Non-Scale Victories

In addition to setting realistic expectations, it is crucial to celebrate non-scale victories along the way. Non-scale victories are achievements that are not directly related to the number on the scale but are still indicators of progress.

These can include things like increased strength, improved endurance, better sleep quality, or increased confidence. By recognizing and celebrating these achievements, you can stay motivated and focused on the positive changes that are happening in your body and overall well-being.

Find Your Why

Understanding your personal motivation for wanting to lose weight can be a powerful tool in staying motivated. Take some time to reflect on why you want to achieve your weight loss goals. Is it to improve your health, boost your self-confidence, or set a positive example for your loved ones?

Whatever your reasons may be, write them down and keep them somewhere visible as a reminder of why you started this journey. When faced with challenges or plateaus, reconnecting with your "why" can provide the motivation and determination needed to keep pushing forward.

Mix Up Your Routine

Plateaus can often occur when your body becomes accustomed to your current exercise and nutrition routine. To overcome these plateaus, it is important to mix up your routine and introduce new challenges to your body.

This can be done by trying different types of workouts, increasing the intensity or duration of your workouts, or incorporating new and exciting healthy recipes into your meal plan. By keeping your body guessing and constantly challenging yourself, you can break through plateaus and continue making progress towards your weight loss goals.

Seek Support and Accountability

Having a support system in place can greatly contribute to your motivation and success in overcoming plateaus. Surround yourself with like-minded individuals who are also on a weight loss journey or seek the guidance of a professional such as a personal trainer or a registered dietitian.

These individuals can provide support, guidance, and accountability, helping you stay motivated and on track. Additionally, consider joining online communities or support groups where you can share your experiences, seek advice, and celebrate your successes with others who understand the challenges of weight loss.

Practice Self-Care

Taking care of your mental and emotional well-being is essential for staying motivated and overcoming plateaus. Incorporate self-care practices into your routine, such as practicing mindfulness or meditation, engaging in activities that bring you joy, getting enough sleep, and managing stress effectively.

When you prioritize self-care, you are better equipped to handle challenges and setbacks, and you are more likely to stay motivated and focused on your weight loss goals.

Track Your Progress

Tracking your progress is an effective way to stay motivated and overcome plateaus. Keep a record of your workouts, meals, and measurements to monitor your progress over time. This can help you identify patterns, make adjustments to your routine if necessary, and celebrate the progress you have made.

Additionally, consider taking progress photos to visually track your transformation. Seeing how far you have come can be incredibly motivating and remind you of the progress you are capable of achieving.

Stay Positive and Practice Gratitude

Maintaining a positive mindset is crucial when facing plateaus and challenges. Instead of focusing on what is not working, shift your focus to what is going well. Practice gratitude by acknowledging the positive changes you have experienced and expressing gratitude for your body's ability to adapt and change. By cultivating a positive mindset and focusing on the progress you have made, you can stay motivated and overcome plateaus with a renewed sense of determination.

Remember, plateaus are a normal part of the weight loss journey. By staying motivated, setting realistic expectations, celebrating non-scale victories, mixing up your routine, seeking support, practicing self-care, tracking your progress, and maintaining a positive mindset, you can overcome plateaus and continue making progress towards your weight loss goals. Stay committed, stay focused, and trust in the process.

You've got this!

Transitioning from Weight Loss to Maintenance

As you transition from weight loss to maintenance, it is crucial to set realistic expectations for yourself. Remember that maintaining your weight loss is a long-term commitment and may require some adjustments along the way. It is normal for your weight to fluctuate slightly, so don't be discouraged if you see small changes on the scale.

Finding Your Maintenance Calorie Intake

During the weight loss phase, you were likely in a calorie deficit, consuming fewer calories than your body needed to maintain its weight. Now that you have reached your goal weight, you will need to determine your maintenance calorie intake. This is the number of calories you need to consume to maintain your current weight.

To find your maintenance calorie intake, you can use online calculators or consult with a registered dietitian. It is important to remember that this number is not set in stone and may need to be adjusted based on your activity level, metabolism, and individual needs.

Building a Sustainable Exercise Routine

Regular physical activity is essential for maintaining weight loss and overall health. As you transition to the maintenance phase, it is important to continue incorporating exercise into your routine. Find activities that you enjoy and that fit into your lifestyle. Aim for a combination of cardiovascular exercise, strength training, and flexibility exercises.

Consider setting new fitness goals to keep yourself motivated and engaged. This could include participating in a charity run, joining a sports team, or trying out new fitness classes. Remember, exercise should be enjoyable and sustainable for the long term.

Mindful Eating and Portion Control

Practicing mindful eating and portion control is crucial for maintaining your weight loss. Pay attention to your hunger and fullness cues, and eat when you are hungry, stopping when you are satisfied. Avoid mindless snacking or eating out of boredom.

Continue to prioritize nutrient-dense foods such as fruits, vegetables, whole grains, lean proteins, and healthy fats. Be mindful of portion sizes and avoid overeating. Consider using smaller plates and bowls to help control portion sizes.

Creating a Supportive Environment

Maintaining weight loss is easier when you have a supportive environment. Surround yourself with people who encourage and support your healthy lifestyle choices. Share your goals with friends and family, and ask for their support in your journey.

Consider joining a support group or finding an accountability partner who shares similar goals. Having someone to share your challenges and successes with can make a big difference in staying on track.

Monitoring Your Progress

Even though you have reached your weight loss goals, it is important to continue monitoring your progress. Regularly check in with yourself and assess how you are feeling physically and emotionally. Keep track of your weight, body measurements, and any changes in your fitness level.

If you notice any significant changes or challenges, don't hesitate to seek support from a healthcare professional or registered dietitian. They can provide guidance and help you navigate any obstacles you may encounter during the maintenance phase.

Staying Motivated and Overcoming Setbacks

Maintaining weight loss can be challenging, and setbacks are a normal part of the process. It is important to stay motivated and focused on your long-term goals. Remind yourself of the progress you have made and the benefits of maintaining a healthy weight.

If you experience a setback, such as a temporary weight gain or a lapse in your healthy habits, don't be too hard on yourself. Instead, use it as an opportunity to learn and grow. Reflect on what may have contributed to the setback and make a plan to get back on track.

Remember, weight loss maintenance is a lifelong journey. Embrace the healthy habits you have developed and continue to prioritize your well-being. With dedication, consistency, and a positive mindset, you can successfully maintain your weight loss and enjoy a healthier, happier life.

Managing Stress and its Impact on Weight

Stress is an inevitable part of life, and it can have a significant impact on our overall well-being, including our weight. When we experience stress, our bodies release cortisol, a hormone that can affect our appetite, metabolism, and fat storage.

If stress becomes chronic or unmanaged, it can lead to weight gain and make it more challenging to achieve our weight loss goals. In this section, we will explore the relationship between stress and weight, as well as strategies to effectively manage stress for successful weight loss.

Understanding the Stress-Weight Connection

Stress triggers a physiological response in our bodies, commonly known as the "fight or flight" response. During this response, cortisol is released, which can increase our appetite and cravings for high-calorie, comfort foods.

Additionally, cortisol can promote the storage of fat, particularly in the abdominal area. This combination of increased calorie intake and enhanced fat storage can contribute to weight gain or hinder weight loss efforts.

Moreover, stress can also impact our behaviors and lifestyle choices. Many individuals turn to food as a coping mechanism when they are stressed, leading to emotional eating. Stress can also disrupt our sleep patterns, decrease our motivation to exercise, and increase our sedentary behaviors. All of these factors can further contribute to weight gain or make it difficult to lose weight.

Effective Stress Management Techniques

Managing stress is crucial for maintaining a healthy weight and overall well-being. By incorporating effective stress management techniques into our daily lives, we can reduce the negative impact of stress on our weight loss journey. Here are some strategies to help you manage stress effectively:

Practice Relaxation Techniques

Engaging in relaxation techniques can help reduce stress levels and promote a sense of calm. Techniques such as deep breathing exercises, meditation, yoga, and progressive muscle relaxation can be highly effective in managing stress. Find a technique that resonates with you and make it a regular part of your routine.

Engage in Regular Physical Activity

Physical activity is not only beneficial for weight loss but also for stress reduction. Exercise releases endorphins, which are natural mood boosters. Regular physical activity can help alleviate stress, improve sleep quality, and enhance overall well-being. Find activities that you enjoy and make them a priority in your daily routine.

Prioritize Self-Care

Taking care of yourself is essential for managing stress. Make time for activities that bring you joy and relaxation, such as reading, taking baths, listening to music, or spending time in nature. Engaging in self-care activities can help reduce stress levels and improve your overall mental and emotional well-being.

Practice Mindfulness

Mindfulness involves being fully present in the moment and non-judgmentally observing your thoughts and feelings. By practicing mindfulness, you can become more aware of your stress triggers and develop healthier ways to cope with them. Mindfulness techniques, such as mindful eating, can also help you make better food choices and prevent emotional eating.

Build a Strong Support System

Having a strong support system can significantly impact your ability to manage stress. Surround yourself with positive and supportive individuals who can provide encouragement, guidance, and understanding. Share your weight loss journey with them and lean on them for support during times of stress.

Get Sufficient Sleep

Sleep plays a vital role in managing stress and maintaining a healthy weight. Lack of sleep can increase cortisol levels and disrupt hunger-regulating hormones, leading to increased appetite and cravings. Aim for seven to nine hours of quality sleep each night to support your weight loss efforts and effectively manage stress.

Incorporating Stress Management into Your Weight Loss Plan

To effectively manage stress and its impact on weight, it is essential to incorporate stress management techniques into your weight loss plan. Here are some tips to help you integrate stress management into your daily routine:

Schedule regular relaxation sessions: Set aside specific times each day for relaxation techniques such as deep breathing exercises, meditation, or yoga.

Plan physical activity: Incorporate regular exercise into your schedule, aiming for at least 150 minutes of moderate-intensity aerobic activity per week. Choose activities that you enjoy and that help you relieve stress.

Prioritize self-care: Make self-care activities a non-negotiable part of your routine. Schedule time for activities that bring you joy and relaxation.

Practice mindful eating: Pay attention to your eating habits and emotions surrounding food. Practice mindful eating by savoring each bite, eating slowly, and listening to your body's hunger and fullness cues.

Seek support: Share your weight loss journey with a supportive friend, family member, or join a support group. Having someone to lean on during times of stress can make a significant difference.

Create a sleep routine: Establish a consistent sleep schedule and create a relaxing bedtime routine to ensure you get sufficient sleep each night.

By incorporating these stress management techniques into your weight loss plan, you can effectively manage stress and create a healthier and more sustainable approach to weight loss.

Remember, managing stress is not only beneficial for weight loss but also for your overall well-being. Prioritize self-care, engage in relaxation techniques, and seek support when needed.

By taking care of your mental and emotional health, you will be better equipped to achieve your weight loss goals and maintain a healthy lifestyle in the long run.

Tracking Progress and Adjusting Your Plan

Tracking your progress is an essential part of any weight loss journey. It allows you to monitor your success, identify areas for improvement, and make necessary adjustments to your plan. By keeping track of your progress, you can stay motivated, stay accountable, and ensure that you are on the right track towards achieving your weight loss goals.

In this section, we will discuss the importance of tracking your progress and provide you with practical tips on how to do it effectively.

Why Tracking Progress is Important

Tracking your progress is crucial because it provides you with tangible evidence of your efforts and helps you stay focused on your goals. It allows you to see how far you have come and provides motivation to keep going. Additionally, tracking your progress can help you identify patterns and trends that may be hindering your progress or contributing to your success.

By monitoring your progress, you can identify what strategies are working for you and what areas need improvement. For example, if you notice that you consistently struggle with late-night snacking, tracking your progress can help you identify this pattern and find ways to address it.

Similarly, if you see that you are consistently losing weight at a slower rate than expected, tracking can help you identify potential reasons and make necessary adjustments to your plan.

Choosing the Right Tracking Method

There are various methods you can use to track your progress, and it's important to choose the one that works best for you. Here are a few popular tracking methods:

Food Diary

Keeping a food diary is a simple yet effective way to track your daily food intake. You can use a notebook, a smartphone app, or an online tool to record everything you eat and drink throughout the day.

Be sure to include portion sizes and any additional information such as the time of day or your emotional state when eating. This method can help you become more aware of your eating habits and identify areas where you can make healthier choices.

Body Measurements

Tracking your body measurements, such as your waist circumference, hip circumference, and body fat percentage, can provide valuable insights into your progress. While the number on the scale may not always accurately reflect your body composition changes, measurements can give you a more comprehensive picture of your progress. Take measurements regularly, preferably once a week, and record them in a journal or a tracking app.

Progress Photos

Taking progress photos can be a powerful way to visually track your transformation. Choose a consistent time and place to take your photos, such as in front of a mirror, and take pictures from different angles.

Compare your photos over time to see the changes in your body shape and overall appearance. Remember to be patient, as progress may not always be visible in the early stages of your weight loss journey.

Fitness and Performance Tracking

If you incorporate exercise into your weight loss plan, tracking your fitness and performance can be highly beneficial. Keep a record of your workouts, including the type of exercise, duration, intensity, and any milestones or personal records you achieve.

This can help you see improvements in your strength, endurance, and overall fitness level, which can be motivating and reinforce your commitment to your weight loss goals.

Setting Realistic Goals and Milestones

When tracking your progress, it's important to set realistic goals and milestones. Setting unrealistic expectations can lead to frustration and disappointment, which may derail your progress. Instead, focus on setting small, achievable goals that are specific, measurable, attainable, relevant, and time-bound (SMART goals).

For example, instead of aiming to lose 20 pounds in a month, set a goal to lose 1-2 pounds per week. This is a more realistic and sustainable approach to weight loss. Celebrate each milestone you achieve along the way, whether it's losing a certain amount of weight, fitting into a smaller clothing size, or reaching a new fitness milestone. These small victories will keep you motivated and reinforce your commitment to your weight loss journey.

Adjusting Your Plan

Tracking your progress allows you to identify areas where your plan may need adjustment. If you find that you are not making progress or are experiencing a plateau, it may be time to reassess your approach. Here are a few strategies to consider when adjusting your plan:

Calorie Intake

If you are not seeing the desired results, you may need to reassess your calorie intake. Ensure that you are in a calorie deficit by consuming fewer calories than your body needs to maintain its current weight. Consider consulting with a registered dietitian or nutritionist to help you determine the appropriate calorie intake for your weight loss goals.

Exercise Routine

If you have been following the same exercise routine for a while and are not seeing progress, it may be time to switch things up. Incorporate different types of exercises, increase the intensity or duration of your workouts, or try new fitness classes or activities. This can help challenge your body and prevent plateaus.

Lifestyle Factors

Consider other lifestyle factors that may be impacting your progress. Are you getting enough sleep? Are you managing stress effectively? Are there any emotional or psychological factors that may be affecting your eating habits? Addressing these factors can help you create a more balanced and sustainable weight loss plan.

Celebrating Non-Scale Victories

While tracking your progress is important, it's equally important to celebrate non-scale victories along the way. Non-scale victories are achievements that are not directly related to the number on the scale but are still significant indicators of progress.

These can include increased energy levels, improved sleep quality, reduced cravings, increased strength or endurance, and improved overall well-being. Acknowledge and celebrate these victories as they are a testament to your hard work and dedication.

Tracking your progress and adjusting your plan accordingly are essential components of a successful weight loss journey. By choosing the right tracking method, setting realistic goals, and making necessary adjustments, you can stay on track towards achieving your weight loss goals.

Remember to celebrate your progress, both on and off the scale, and stay committed to creating a healthier and happier version of yourself.

Stay trim.

Also by Tiwayi Mushambi

The First Victory - The Power of Self-Discipline
It's Not Easy, But It's Simple
Fret Not: A Comprehensive Guide To Taming Your Anxiety
Vice Grip: Understanding and Overcoming Addiction
Money Mastery: The Ultimate Guide to Financial Discipline
Trim The Fat: Weight Loss Simplified

www.ingramcontent.com/pod-product-compliance
Lightning Source LLC
Chambersburg PA
CBHW071240130726

47998CB00003B/1016